Soar

Indie Author Business Planner

Second Edition

Name _____

Address _____

_____

_____

_____

© 2022 Delia Remington

Delia Remington

Soar: Indie Author Business Planner

All rights reserved. No part of this publication may be reproduced, stored in a retrieval system or transmitted in any form or by any means, electronic, mechanical, photocopying, recording or otherwise without the prior permission of the publisher or in accordance with the provisions of the Copyright, Designs and Patents Act 1988 or under the terms of any license permitting limited copying issued by the Copyright Licensing Agency. Please purchase only authorized electronic editions, and do not participate in or encourage electronic piracy of copyrighted materials. Thank you for your support of the author's rights.

Eagle Heights Press
414 N. Church St.
Fayette, MO 65248
eagleheightspress.com

First Edition: June 2019
Second Edition: August 2022

Eagle Heights Press is a division of Eagle Heights L.L.C.

The publisher is not responsible for websites (or their content) that are not owned by the publisher.

Published by: Eagle Heights Press

ISBN-13: 978-1-947181-17-5

Printed in the United States of America

Soar

INDIE AUTHOR BUSINESS PLANNER

SECOND EDITION

A Twelve-Month Guide to Helping
Your Indie Publishing Business Take Flight

EAGLEHEIGHTSPRESS

Also by Delia Remington

The Blood Royal Saga
Vampire Series
In The Blood
Out For Blood
Trial By Blood

Introduction

Writing was always something I did for fun. I wrote in stolen moments, never intending to share those words with anyone but myself and a few close friends. When I decided to try turning my hobby into a career, however, I quickly discovered that while it was easy to find a plethora of information on writing and the technical aspects of indie publishing, I didn't know how to organize my time and plan the business aspects of the job.

While small business planners are abundant, none of them were tailored to being an indie author. As a result, for the first year, I floundered with inadequate organizational tools, moving forward by guesswork rather than design. Each claimed to be a "one-sized-fits-all" solution, but the reality was anything but. Instead, I spent my time frustratedly shuttling between a variety of schedule books and business planners, none of which were ideal for me.

Then I found bullet journals, and I thought I had found nirvana. Here was a blank slate that allowed me to create the planner of my dreams. I read tons of books and blogs, full of amazing suggestions. I loved the minimalism and flexibility of the method. It's also wonderful as a creative outlet. I'm an amateur calligrapher and enjoyed decorating each page with colorful washi tape and doodling.

However, as my days grew busier, those beautiful handmade page layouts became time consuming and burdensome to generate. Once again, I longed for a planner that would give me the author-specific tools I needed and yet allow for some creative flexibility. I wanted to reclaim my time so I could spend it doing what made me love what I do in the first place. That meant I needed to return to using a printed planner.

At first, I created these pages for myself. They're modeled on the pages I have been using in my bullet journal. I combined what works for me in organizing my business growth into clean, easy to use templates. However, I'm not giving you a one-size-fits-all planner. I know that everyone has different needs.

I have left room for you to make this tool your own. You don't have to wait until January first to begin using this book. You can begin where you are with a twelve month set of pages that will help you plan your future career. There are also some dotted pages included in each month's pages so you can create trackers or layouts tailored to your specific needs. And if you enjoy the creative aspect of bullet journals, every page is dotted so you can customize them to suit your decorative taste.

In this first portion of the book, I will explain how to use the pages with specific examples from my own planner, give you the tools to plan the next twelve months of your life, and explain how to break down big annual goals into quarterly, monthly, weekly, and daily tasks to help you achieve your dreams. At the end, I'll guide you through an annual review and help you keep the momentum going.

I hope I've created a planner that is the best of both worlds. I also hope this book takes some of the fear and stress out of the business management aspects of being an indie author and helps you spend more productive time doing what you love.

Make this book yours, and soar to success!

    Best wishes,

Delia Remington

How This Book Works

I've written this planner so it can be used right away, regardless of whether it's January 1 or August 21. The calendars and weekly spread pages are deliberately designed without dates so you can customize them, no matter when you start.

Whether you're pursuing writing on a full time or part time basis, you should be able to tailor this book to suit your needs. Whatever genre or word count you prefer, this book is designed to help you juggle all the tasks life throws at you.

The planning pages are designed to help you turn your big picture dream into actionable steps. First, you'll determine your annual plan, then you'll decide in which quarter you'll tackle the steps required. You'll break down those steps into monthly goals. You'll divide those monthly goals into weekly tasks, and then on your weekly spreads you'll make a bullet list of daily assignments you can check off.

Along the way, you'll record your weekly progress and gratitude and give yourself monthly and quarterly assessments to help you make adjustments and improvements as you work.

Finally, there's an annual review to help you take note of all you accomplished and to begin planning for the next year.

Ready to dive in? Let's get to it!

ANNUAL PLAN

You can't get where you're going if you don't have an idea of your destination.

Don't be afraid to think big. This is your place to dream. No one else has to see this but you, so let's establish some things you wish you could do.

Set aside twenty five minutes to work on each section without distractions. Use a timer or an alarm on your phone, and let's get to work!

1. Shift your thoughts to the end of your life as though you're looking back on all you've done. What would you like to have people say about you? What would you like to be remembered for?

2. Why do these things matter to you?

3. Think about what kind of person you'd have to become in order to accomplish those things. Who is that person? Describe the life you'd like to be living.

4. Who are your mentors and role models? What attributes of their lives would you like to incorporate into your own? Why?

---
5 MINUTE BREAK

Look over your life goals, and then think about the path that will lead you there.

1. Where would you need to be in 10 years in order to make that happen?

2. Five years?

3. Three years?

---
5 MINUTE BREAK

Soar

Now let's get more specific.

1. Where would you like to be at this time next year? List the things you want to be able to say you've accomplished, not just in your career but in all aspects of your life.

2. How would your life be different if those dreams came true? Really take time to envision and describe those changes in as much detail as possible.

3. If you knew you were unstoppable, what would you do?

4. How will you know if you've made it? What does "success" look like?

5. What will accomplishing those dreams mean for your future?

Soar

---
15 MINUTE BREAK - Get up, stretch, take a walk, get a drink of water, then come back when you're fresh and rested.

Keeping in mind those big picture ideas for next year, think about your life as it is currently.

1. What needs to change in your financial life? Why?

2. What needs to change in your relationship with friends and family? Why?

3. What needs to change in your physical and mental health? Why?

---
5 MINUTE BREAK

Now let's visualize how making those changes will help those dreams manifest in all parts of your life.

1. How is your financial situation different?

2. How are your relationships different?

3. How has your physical and mental health improved?

---
5 MINUTE BREAK

Look back over where you are compared to where you'd like to be.

1. What actions do you need to take in order to make the changes in your life you've outlined?

2. What do you need to learn? How will you go about getting that training, skill, and practice?

3. What will you have to give up? Bad habits? Sacrifices?

4. Celebrating small successes is key to staying motivated. How will you reward yourself for the steps toward those changes?

5. What will you do when things don't go according to plan? How will you get back on track?

---

15 MINUTE BREAK - Get up, stretch, take a walk, get a drink of water, then come back when you're fresh and rested.

Now that you know the big picture, let's get more specific.

Being an indie author means wearing several hats. I often joke that I feel like Dick Van Dyke and his one man band in Mary Poppins, playing all the instruments simultaneously. I am not just a writer. I'm an editor, proofreader, formatter, graphic designer, publicist, marketing director, social media guru, web designer, sales manager, bookkeeper, and public speaker. I am also a member of several professional organizations, and I make sure to get an adequate amount of continuing education in all these areas in order to stay up to date and improve my performance. I'm learning about podcasting and video production. And finally, as the owner of my publishing business, I'm my own boss, so that means I have to oversee and evaluate my own work performance and manage my own assignments.

You may hire out some of these tasks or you may have an agent or publisher who takes some of these jobs off your plate, but you still have to keep these various categories of work in mind throughout the year so nothing slips through the cracks and is left undone. My way to stay on top of all these components of the job is to have a Division of Labor chart so I can track my progress. I begin by doing some brainstorming, so that's what I'm going to ask you to do now.

In the chart below, list all the various types of tasks you know need to be done this year in order to achieve your annual plan. I've left a few blank sections for other tasks you might do. Under "Writing," list the projects you have in mind. Place a star next to the tasks you think you need to learn more about in order to be truly competent at the job. Place a letter H next to any items you might need to hire someone to help you complete.

Writing	Graphics
Editing/Proofreading	Social Media
Blogging	Public Speaking/Publicity

Soar

Web Design	Sales
Marketing	Advertising
Bookkeeping	Professional Organizations
Continuing Education	Podcasting

Soar

5 MINUTE BREAK

Now that you know the types of tasks you need to tackle, you're ready to make a plan. Let's visualize what a typical writing workday looks like. In order to succeed, you need to treat it like a job. Setting a schedule helps you manage expectations and get into a groove. Think about what habits you can implement into your daily routine to help you stay on track and visualize what it looks like when you're productive.

1. What time of day works best for you? Are you a night person or a day person? Do you have family obligations that dictate your schedule? Do you have another job that determines when you have time to focus on your writing life?

2. Where do you work? Do you have a home office? A designated space for writing? Or do you need to go to a coffee shop or library to get away from distractions in your home?

3. Do you work best with music? With silence? Would noise canceling headphones help?

4. How are you dressed for work?

5. How many hours a day do you work? What's your method of making that time productive?

6. Do you work better writing by hand? Typing? Dictating? Does it vary depending on the situation?

7. What do your breaks look like? How often do you take them? What do you do to refresh your mind and body so you can maintain focus? Meditation? Yoga? Exercise?

8. How will you maintain a healthy work/life balance? What strategies will you use in order to stave off burnout?

9. How will you incorporate those routines when you're away from home?

Soar

5 MINUTE BREAK

Now that you've determined what your daily routine needs to look like in order to be productive, decide how you're going to make sure that routine isn't interrupted. That means establishing "office hours" and letting the important people in your life know what you're doing and why.

This establishes expectations with them and helps reduce friction when their wishes come into conflict with your needs.

1. How will you explain your needs to your family?

2. What potential issues do you worry your family might have with your routine?

3. What can you do to resolve those conflicts before they blow up?

4. How will you explain your needs to your friends?

5. Are they supportive of your choices?

6. How will you resolve potential conflicts?

---
15 MINUTE BREAK - Get up, stretch, take a walk, get a drink of water, then come back when you're fresh and rested.

Soar

Awesome! You're ready now to create an action plan. Turn back to the Division of Labor chart. Let's break up that work into quarters.

Quarter 1:

Quarter 2:

Soar

Don't worry about trying to get it in order here. We're just broadly sorting.

Quarter 3:

Quarter 4:

Soar

5 MINUTE BREAK

Let's break it down further using the rest of the planner tools.

1. Turn to the first **Quarterly Rapid Log** and write down the items you listed for Quarter 1.
   Example:

   ### QUARTERLY RAPID LOG:
   - Update Author Website
   - Create new bookmark graphics
   - Place orders for bookmarks and miniflyers
   - Contact Ann from Central Library about reading
   - Search for conventions/events in August
   - Write 10,000 wds./wk
   - TAXES!
   - FB & Twitter ads to run two weeks before book release
   - Make final proofreading correction edits and upload files
   - Finish online public speaking course

2. Now organize your rapid log list using the **Quarterly Progress Log**.
   Example:

   ### QUARTERLY PROGRESS LOG

Writing • Write 10,000 wds./wk	Editing/Proofreading • Make final proofreading correction edits and upload files
Social Media	Graphics • Create new bookmark graphics
Public Speaking/Publicity • Contact Ann from Central Library about reading	Web Design • Update Author Website
Marketing • Place orders for bookmarks and miniflyers	Advertising • FB & Twitter ads to run two weeks before book release
Bookkeeping • TAXES!	Professional Organizations
Continuing Education • Finish online public speaking course	Podcasting
Blogging	Sales • Search for conventions/events in August

3. Once those are written down, you'll use the **Monthly Business Planning** page to give yourself a task list for each of those goals.

   What tasks are still *Open* from the previous month? What jobs are *Closed*? What's *New* business?

Example:

MONTHLY BUSINESS PLANNING

TASKS AND TO-DO LIST:

Open:

- *Update Author Website*
- *TAXES!*
- *Write 10,000 wds./wk*
- *Online public speaking course*

Closed:

- *Cover design for Book 3*
- *Proofread print proof of Book 3*
- *Writer's Guild Convention*
- *New Marketing Banner*

New:

- *Contact Ann from Central Library about reading*
- *Write review for Jeff and submit by the 15th*
- *Research Scottish werewolf myths*

4. On the **Monthly Task** page, you'll assign the task list items to a specific week. This page reflects your goals, and the task assignments may need revision as you go on. Don't worry about getting too far ahead of yourself. Remember that plans need to have some flexibility. Set some *Challenges* for the month and plan some *Rewards* you'll give yourself for completion. Give yourself one task that's a *Bonus* as a stretch goal.

Example:

MONTHLY TASKS TO COMPLETE

WEEK 1	WEEK 2	WEEK 3
• Update Author Website • Make appt. with accountant • Gather annual receipts • Write 10,000 wds. • Online course - Lesson 1-2 • Email Ann at Central Library	• Write 10,000 wds. • Check PayPal sales record • Online course - Lesson 3-4	• Write 10,000 wds. • Online course - Lesson 4-5 • File taxes with accountant • Send off sales tax • Review due for Jeff
WEEK 4	**WEEK 5**	
• Write 10,000 wds. • Online course - Lesson 6-8 • Research Scottish werewolves	• Write 10,000 wds. • Online course - Lesson 19-10	Challenges: • Taxes paid on time • Review submitted • Weekly word count • Online course done by end of month Rewards: • Library day out for every challenge completed Bonus: • Write an extra 5000 words = Binge watch Sabrina

5. And finally, on your **Weekly Spreads**, you'll list those task assignments and then determine which day you'll work on getting them done!
Example:

WEEKLY TASK LIST

Monthly Plan:
- Update Author Website
- Make appt. with accountant
- Gather annual receipts
- Write 10,000 wds.
- Online course - Lesson 1-2
- Email Ann at Central Library

Life Duties:
- Laundry
- Groceries
- Turn over compost
- Meal prep on Sunday
- Ladies Day out with Mom?
- Dogs to groomer

WEEKLY SPREAD

Monday Date 6	Tuesday Date 7
• Make appt. with accountant • Gather annual receipts • Write 2,000 wds. • Email Ann at Central Library	• Update Author Website • Write 2,000 wds. • Trash day • Laundry

Wednesday Date 8	Thursday Date 9
• Write 2,000 wds. • Online course - Lesson 1 • Dogs to groomer 8am	• Ladies Day out with Mom • Library • Grocery shopping

Friday Date 10	Saturday Date 11
• Write 2,000 wds. • Online course - Lesson 2	• Write 2,000 wds. • Turn over compost

Sunday Date 12	DAILY SCORECARD
• If word count is complete, RELAX • Meal prep evening	M ○○○○ T ○○○○ W ○○○○ T ○○○○ F ○○○○ S ○○○○ S ○○○○

Rate your daily progress

Soar

Congratulations!

You have an action plan for the year. Now you're ready to go accomplish your goals and make your dreams come true!

Final Notes on this Planner

There are daily, weekly, monthly, quarterly, and annual assessments to keep you on track. Use these to help you pay attention to what's going well and adapt when things don't go according to plan.

Also included in this book is a **Master Events Calendar** so you can keep track of major life and work events throughout the year all on one two-page spread. This makes it easy to schedule conventions, book events, family vacations, or whatever else is most important to you.

Monthly pages also include **habit trackers** where you can track behavior you want to encourage. I use mine to remind myself to take my vitamins, to meditate, to do 30 minutes of walking, and to complete my daily word count.

Finally, there are **blank pages** incorporated throughout the book so you can take notes, make plans, doodle, or whatever else you want your planner to help you do. I've made those pages dotted so you can use them like bullet journal sheets.

With that, you're ready to *Soar!*

Soar

MASTER EVENTS CALENDAR

January	February	March

July	August	September

Soar

April	May	June
October	November	December

Soar

Soar

Soar

QUARTERLY RAPID LOG:

Soar

QUARTERLY PROGRESS LOG

Writing	Editing/Proofreading
Social Media	Graphics
Public Speaking/Publicity	Web Design
Marketing	Advertising
Bookkeeping	Professional Organizations
Continuing Education	Podcasting
Blogging	Sales

Soar

GOALS for the Month of _____

Work	Health	Self-Care

Creativity	Relationships	Household To-Dos

Soar

Monday	Tuesday	Wednesday	Thursday	Friday	Saturday	Sunday
○	○	○	○	○	○	○
○	○	○	○	○	○	○
○	○	○	○	○	○	○
○	○	○	○	○	○	○
○	○	○	○	○	○	○
○	○	○	○	○	○	○

Habit	1	2	3	4	5	6	7	8	9	10	11	12	13	14	15	16	17	18	19	20	21	22	23	24	25	26	27	28	29	30	31

Soar

Monthly Business Planning

Tasks and To-Do List:

Open:

Closed:

New:

Soar

MONTHLY TASKS TO COMPLETE

WEEK 1	WEEK 2	WEEK 3
WEEK 4	**WEEK 5**	**WEEK 6**

Challenges: Rewards: Bonus:

Soar

WEEKLY SPREAD

Monday Date _____	Tuesday Date _____

Wednesday Date _____	Thursday Date _____

Friday Date _____	Saturday Date _____

Sunday Date _____	**DAILY SCORECARD**
	1 2 3 4 M ○ ○ ○ ○ T ○ ○ ○ ○ W ○ ○ ○ ○ T ○ ○ ○ ○ F ○ ○ ○ ○ S ○ ○ ○ ○ S ○ ○ ○ ○

Soar

Weekly Task List

Monthly Plan: Life Duties:

Gratitude

Weekly Assessment

Weekly Achievements:	What problems arose?
What worked well?	What needs adjustment?

Soar

WEEKLY SPREAD

Monday Date _____	Tuesday Date _____

Wednesday Date _____	Thursday Date _____

Friday Date _____	Saturday Date _____

Sunday Date _____	**DAILY SCORECARD**
	1 2 3 4 M ○ ○ ○ ○ T ○ ○ ○ ○ W ○ ○ ○ ○ T ○ ○ ○ ○ F ○ ○ ○ ○ S ○ ○ ○ ○ S ○ ○ ○ ○

Soar

Weekly Task List

Monthly Plan:

Life Duties:

Gratitude

Weekly Assessment

Weekly Achievements:	What problems arose?
What worked well?	What needs adjustment?

Soar

WEEKLY SPREAD

Monday Date _____	Tuesday Date _____

Wednesday Date _____	Thursday Date _____

Friday Date _____	Saturday Date _____

Sunday Date _____	**DAILY SCORECARD**
	1 2 3 4 M ○○○○ T ○○○○ W ○○○○ T ○○○○ F ○○○○ S ○○○○ S ○○○○

Soar

Weekly Task List

Monthly Plan: Life Duties:

Gratitude

Weekly Assessment

Weekly Achievements:	What problems arose?
What worked well?	What needs adjustment?

Soar

WEEKLY SPREAD

Monday Date _____	Tuesday Date _____

Wednesday Date _____	Thursday Date _____

Friday Date _____	Saturday Date _____

Sunday Date _____	**DAILY SCORECARD**
	1 2 3 4 M ○ ○ ○ ○ T ○ ○ ○ ○ W ○ ○ ○ ○ T ○ ○ ○ ○ F ○ ○ ○ ○ S ○ ○ ○ ○ S ○ ○ ○ ○

Soar

Weekly Task List

Monthly Plan:

Life Duties:

Gratitude

Weekly Assessment

Weekly Achievements:

What problems arose?

What worked well?

What needs adjustment?

Soar

WEEKLY SPREAD

Monday Date _____	Tuesday Date _____

Wednesday Date _____	Thursday Date _____

Friday Date _____	Saturday Date _____

Sunday Date _____	**DAILY SCORECARD**
	1 2 3 4 M ○○○○ T ○○○○ W ○○○○ T ○○○○ F ○○○○ S ○○○○ S ○○○○

Soar

Weekly Task List

Monthly Plan:

Life Duties:

Gratitude

Weekly Assessment

Weekly Achievements:	What problems arose?
What worked well?	What needs adjustment?

Soar

WEEKLY SPREAD

Monday Date _____	Tuesday Date _____

Wednesday Date _____	Thursday Date _____

Friday Date _____	Saturday Date _____

Sunday Date _____	**DAILY SCORECARD**
	1 2 3 4 M ○ ○ ○ ○ T ○ ○ ○ ○ W ○ ○ ○ ○ T ○ ○ ○ ○ F ○ ○ ○ ○ S ○ ○ ○ ○ S ○ ○ ○ ○

Soar

WEEKLY TASK LIST

Monthly Plan: Life Duties:

Gratitude

WEEKLY ASSESSMENT

Weekly Achievements:	What problems arose?
What worked well?	What needs adjustment?

Soar

MONTHLY REVIEW for the Month of _____

Social Media Follower Count Growth Tracker:
Facebook   Instagram   Twitter   Website   Pinterest   _____   _____   _____
_____   _____   _____   _____   _____   _____   _____

Sales Tracker:
Income: Salary: Expenses: Profit:

Total Earned (Year-to-Date):

Completed:	Am I closer to my annual goals?	Obstacles:
	If yes, how will I keep going?	
		What are the causes?
	If not, what will I change?	
Still in the Works:		What solutions have I tried?
	What worked well?	
		What else could I try?
	How can I continue?	

Notes and Planning

Soar

Soar

Soar

Soar

GOALS for the Month of _____

Work	Health	Self-Care

Creativity	Relationships	Household To-Dos

Soar

Monday	Tuesday	Wednesday	Thursday	Friday	Saturday	Sunday
○	○	○	○	○	○	○
○	○	○	○	○	○	○
○	○	○	○	○	○	○
○	○	○	○	○	○	○
○	○	○	○	○	○	○
○	○	○	○	○	○	○

Habit	1	2	3	4	5	6	7	8	9	10	11	12	13	14	15	16	17	18	19	20	21	22	23	24	25	26	27	28	29	30	31

Soar

MONTHLY BUSINESS PLANNING

TASKS AND TO-DO LIST:

Open:

Closed:

New:

Soar

MONTHLY TASKS TO COMPLETE

Week 1	Week 2	Week 3

Week 4	Week 5	Week 6

Challenges: Rewards: Bonus:

Soar

WEEKLY SPREAD

Monday Date _____	Tuesday Date _____

Wednesday Date _____	Thursday Date _____

Friday Date _____	Saturday Date _____

Sunday Date _____	**DAILY SCORECARD**
	1 2 3 4 M ○ ○ ○ ○ T ○ ○ ○ ○ W ○ ○ ○ ○ T ○ ○ ○ ○ F ○ ○ ○ ○ S ○ ○ ○ ○ S ○ ○ ○ ○

Soar

Weekly Task List

Monthly Plan:

Life Duties:

Gratitude

Weekly Assessment

Weekly Achievements:

What problems arose?

What worked well?

What needs adjustment?

Soar

WEEKLY SPREAD

Monday Date _____	Tuesday Date _____
Wednesday Date _____	Thursday Date _____
Friday Date _____	Saturday Date _____
Sunday Date _____	**DAILY SCORECARD**

Daily Scorecard

	1	2	3	4
M	○	○	○	○
T	○	○	○	○
W	○	○	○	○
T	○	○	○	○
F	○	○	○	○
S	○	○	○	○
S	○	○	○	○

Soar

Weekly Task List

Monthly Plan:

Life Duties:

Gratitude

Weekly Assessment

Weekly Achievements:	What problems arose?
What worked well?	What needs adjustment?

Soar

WEEKLY SPREAD

Monday Date _____	Tuesday Date _____

Wednesday Date _____	Thursday Date _____

Friday Date _____	Saturday Date _____

Sunday Date _____	**DAILY SCORECARD**
	1 2 3 4 M ○ ○ ○ ○ T ○ ○ ○ ○ W ○ ○ ○ ○ T ○ ○ ○ ○ F ○ ○ ○ ○ S ○ ○ ○ ○ S ○ ○ ○ ○

Soar

Weekly Task List

Monthly Plan:

Life Duties:

Gratitude

Weekly Assessment

Weekly Achievements:	What problems arose?
What worked well?	What needs adjustment?

Soar

WEEKLY SPREAD

Monday Date _____	Tuesday Date _____

Wednesday Date _____	Thursday Date _____

Friday Date _____	Saturday Date _____

Sunday Date _____	**DAILY SCORECARD**
	1 2 3 4 M ○ ○ ○ ○ T ○ ○ ○ ○ W ○ ○ ○ ○ T ○ ○ ○ ○ F ○ ○ ○ ○ S ○ ○ ○ ○ S ○ ○ ○ ○

Soar

Weekly Task List

Monthly Plan:

Life Duties:

Gratitude

Weekly Assessment

Weekly Achievements:

What problems arose?

What worked well?

What needs adjustment?

Soar

WEEKLY SPREAD

Monday Date _____	Tuesday Date _____

Wednesday Date _____	Thursday Date _____

Friday Date _____	Saturday Date _____

Sunday Date _____	**DAILY SCORECARD**
	1 2 3 4 M ○ ○ ○ ○ T ○ ○ ○ ○ W ○ ○ ○ ○ T ○ ○ ○ ○ F ○ ○ ○ ○ S ○ ○ ○ ○ S ○ ○ ○ ○

Weekly Task List

Monthly Plan:	Life Duties:

Gratitude

Weekly Assessment

Weekly Achievements:	What problems arose?
What worked well?	What needs adjustment?

Soar

WEEKLY SPREAD

Monday Date _____	Tuesday Date _____
Wednesday Date _____	Thursday Date _____
Friday Date _____	Saturday Date _____
Sunday Date _____	**DAILY SCORECARD** 　　　　1 2 3 4 M ○ ○ ○ ○ T ○ ○ ○ ○ W ○ ○ ○ ○ T ○ ○ ○ ○ F ○ ○ ○ ○ S ○ ○ ○ ○ S ○ ○ ○ ○

Soar

WEEKLY TASK LIST

Monthly Plan: Life Duties:

Gratitude

WEEKLY ASSESSMENT

Weekly Achievements:	What problems arose?
What worked well?	What needs adjustment?

Soar

MONTHLY REVIEW for the Month of _____

Social Media Follower Count Growth Tracker:
Facebook   Instagram   Twitter   Website   Pinterest   _____   _____   _____

_____   _____   _____   _____   _____   _____   _____

Sales Tracker:
Income: Salary: Expenses: Profit:

Total Earned (Year-to-Date):

Completed:	Am I closer to my annual goals?	Obstacles:
	If yes, how will I keep going?	
		What are the causes?
	If not, what will I change?	
Still in the Works:		What solutions have I tried?
	What worked well?	
		What else could I try?
	How can I continue?	

NOTES AND PLANNING

Soar

Soar

Soar

Soar

GOALS for the Month of _____

Work	Health	Self-Care

Creativity	Relationships	Household To-Dos

Soar

Monday	Tuesday	Wednesday	Thursday	Friday	Saturday	Sunday
○	○	○	○	○	○	○
○	○	○	○	○	○	○
○	○	○	○	○	○	○
○	○	○	○	○	○	○
○	○	○	○	○	○	○
○	○	○	○	○	○	○

Habit	1	2	3	4	5	6	7	8	9	10	11	12	13	14	15	16	17	18	19	20	21	22	23	24	25	26	27	28	29	30	31

Soar

MONTHLY BUSINESS PLANNING

TASKS AND TO-DO LIST:

Open:

Closed:

New:

Soar

Monthly Tasks to Complete

Week 1	Week 2	Week 3

Week 4	Week 5	Week 6

Challenges:

Rewards:

Bonus:

Soar

WEEKLY SPREAD

Monday Date _____	Tuesday Date _____
Wednesday Date _____	Thursday Date _____
Friday Date _____	Saturday Date _____
Sunday Date _____	**DAILY SCORECARD** 1 2 3 4 M ○ ○ ○ ○ T ○ ○ ○ ○ W ○ ○ ○ ○ T ○ ○ ○ ○ F ○ ○ ○ ○ S ○ ○ ○ ○ S ○ ○ ○ ○

Soar

WEEKLY TASK LIST

Monthly Plan: Life Duties:

Gratitude

WEEKLY ASSESSMENT

Weekly Achievements: What problems arose?

What worked well?   What needs adjustment?

Soar

WEEKLY SPREAD

Monday Date _____	Tuesday Date _____

Wednesday Date _____	Thursday Date _____

Friday Date _____	Saturday Date _____

Sunday Date _____	**DAILY SCORECARD**
	1 2 3 4 M ○ ○ ○ ○ T ○ ○ ○ ○ W ○ ○ ○ ○ T ○ ○ ○ ○ F ○ ○ ○ ○ S ○ ○ ○ ○ S ○ ○ ○ ○

Soar

WEEKLY TASK LIST

Monthly Plan: Life Duties:

Gratitude

WEEKLY ASSESSMENT

Weekly Achievements:	What problems arose?
What worked well?	What needs adjustment?

Soar

WEEKLY SPREAD

Monday Date _____	Tuesday Date _____
Wednesday Date _____	Thursday Date _____
Friday Date _____	Saturday Date _____
Sunday Date _____	**DAILY SCORECARD**
	1 2 3 4 M ○ ○ ○ ○ T ○ ○ ○ ○ W ○ ○ ○ ○ T ○ ○ ○ ○ F ○ ○ ○ ○ S ○ ○ ○ ○ S ○ ○ ○ ○

Soar

WEEKLY TASK LIST

Monthly Plan:					Life Duties:

Gratitude

WEEKLY ASSESSMENT

Weekly Achievements:	What problems arose?
What worked well?	What needs adjustment?

Soar

WEEKLY SPREAD

Monday Date _____	Tuesday Date _____

Wednesday Date _____	Thursday Date _____

Friday Date _____	Saturday Date _____

Sunday Date _____	**DAILY SCORECARD**
	1 2 3 4 M ○ ○ ○ ○ T ○ ○ ○ ○ W ○ ○ ○ ○ T ○ ○ ○ ○ F ○ ○ ○ ○ S ○ ○ ○ ○ S ○ ○ ○ ○

Soar

WEEKLY TASK LIST

Monthly Plan: Life Duties:

Gratitude

WEEKLY ASSESSMENT

Weekly Achievements:	What problems arose?
What worked well?	What needs adjustment?

Soar

WEEKLY SPREAD

Monday Date _____	Tuesday Date _____
Wednesday Date _____	Thursday Date _____
Friday Date _____	Saturday Date _____
Sunday Date _____	**DAILY SCORECARD**
	1 2 3 4 M ○○○○ T ○○○○ W ○○○○ T ○○○○ F ○○○○ S ○○○○ S ○○○○

Soar

WEEKLY TASK LIST

Monthly Plan:

Life Duties:

Gratitude

WEEKLY ASSESSMENT

Weekly Achievements:	What problems arose?
What worked well?	What needs adjustment?

Soar

WEEKLY SPREAD

Monday Date _____	Tuesday Date _____

Wednesday Date _____	Thursday Date _____

Friday Date _____	Saturday Date _____

Sunday Date _____	**DAILY SCORECARD**
	1 2 3 4 M ○○○○ T ○○○○ W ○○○○ T ○○○○ F ○○○○ S ○○○○ S ○○○○

Soar

WEEKLY TASK LIST

Monthly Plan: Life Duties:

Gratitude

WEEKLY ASSESSMENT

Weekly Achievements: What problems arose?

What worked well?   What needs adjustment?

Soar

MONTHLY REVIEW for the Month of _____

Social Media Follower Count Growth Tracker:
Facebook   Instagram   Twitter   Website   Pinterest   ____   ____   ____
____   ____   ____   ____   ____   ____   ____   ____

Sales Tracker:
Income: Salary: Expenses: Profit:

Total Earned (Year-to-Date):

Completed:	Am I closer to my annual goals?	Obstacles:
	If yes, how will I keep going?	
		What are the causes?
	If not, what will I change?	
Still in the Works:		What solutions have I tried?
	What worked well?	
		What else could I try?
	How can I continue?	

Notes and Planning

Soar

Soar

Soar

Soar

Quarterly Rapid Log:

Quarterly Progress Log

Writing	Editing/Proofreading
Social Media	Graphics
Public Speaking/Publicity	Web Design
Marketing	Advertising
Bookkeeping	Professional Organizations
Continuing Education	Podcasting
Blogging	Sales

Soar

GOALS for the Month of _____

Work	Health	Self-Care

Creativity	Relationships	Household To-Dos

Soar

Monday	Tuesday	Wednesday	Thursday	Friday	Saturday	Sunday
○	○	○	○	○	○	○
○	○	○	○	○	○	○
○	○	○	○	○	○	○
○	○	○	○	○	○	○
○	○	○	○	○	○	○
○	○	○	○	○	○	○

Habit	1	2	3	4	5	6	7	8	9	10	11	12	13	14	15	16	17	18	19	20	21	22	23	24	25	26	27	28	29	30	31

Soar

Monthly Business Planning

Tasks and To-Do List:

Open:

Closed:

New:

Soar

MONTHLY TASKS TO COMPLETE

WEEK 1	WEEK 2	WEEK 3
WEEK 4	**WEEK 5**	**WEEK 6**

Challenges: Rewards: Bonus:

Soar

WEEKLY SPREAD

Monday Date _____	Tuesday Date _____

Wednesday Date _____	Thursday Date _____

Friday Date _____	Saturday Date _____

Sunday Date _____	**DAILY SCORECARD**
	1 2 3 4 M ○ ○ ○ ○ T ○ ○ ○ ○ W ○ ○ ○ ○ T ○ ○ ○ ○ F ○ ○ ○ ○ S ○ ○ ○ ○ S ○ ○ ○ ○

Soar

WEEKLY TASK LIST

Monthly Plan: Life Duties:

Gratitude

WEEKLY ASSESSMENT

Weekly Achievements:	What problems arose?
What worked well?	What needs adjustment?

Soar

WEEKLY SPREAD

Monday Date _____	Tuesday Date _____

Wednesday Date _____	Thursday Date _____

Friday Date _____	Saturday Date _____

Sunday Date _____	**DAILY SCORECARD**
	1 2 3 4 M ○ ○ ○ ○ T ○ ○ ○ ○ W ○ ○ ○ ○ T ○ ○ ○ ○ F ○ ○ ○ ○ S ○ ○ ○ ○ S ○ ○ ○ ○

Soar

WEEKLY TASK LIST

Monthly Plan: Life Duties:

Gratitude

WEEKLY ASSESSMENT

Weekly Achievements:	What problems arose?
What worked well?	What needs adjustment?

Soar

WEEKLY SPREAD

Monday Date _____	Tuesday Date _____
Wednesday Date _____	Thursday Date _____
Friday Date _____	Saturday Date _____
Sunday Date _____	**DAILY SCORECARD**

DAILY SCORECARD

```
    1 2 3 4
M   O O O O
T   O O O O
W   O O O O
T   O O O O
F   O O O O
S   O O O O
S   O O O O
```

Soar

Weekly Task List

Monthly Plan:

Life Duties:

Gratitude

Weekly Assessment

Weekly Achievements:	What problems arose?
What worked well?	What needs adjustment?

Soar

WEEKLY SPREAD

Monday Date _____	Tuesday Date _____

Wednesday Date _____	Thursday Date _____

Friday Date _____	Saturday Date _____

Sunday Date _____	**DAILY SCORECARD**
	1 2 3 4 M ○○○○ T ○○○○ W ○○○○ T ○○○○ F ○○○○ S ○○○○ S ○○○○

Soar

WEEKLY TASK LIST

Monthly Plan:						Life Duties:

Gratitude

WEEKLY ASSESSMENT

Weekly Achievements:	What problems arose?
What worked well?	What needs adjustment?

Soar

WEEKLY SPREAD

Monday Date _____	Tuesday Date _____
Wednesday Date _____	Thursday Date _____
Friday Date _____	Saturday Date _____
Sunday Date _____	**DAILY SCORECARD**

DAILY SCORECARD

   1 2 3 4

M ○ ○ ○ ○
T ○ ○ ○ ○
W ○ ○ ○ ○
T ○ ○ ○ ○
F ○ ○ ○ ○
S ○ ○ ○ ○
S ○ ○ ○ ○

Soar

WEEKLY TASK LIST

Monthly Plan: Life Duties:

Gratitude

WEEKLY ASSESSMENT

Weekly Achievements:	What problems arose?
What worked well?	What needs adjustment?

Soar

WEEKLY SPREAD

Monday Date _____	Tuesday Date _____

Wednesday Date _____	Thursday Date _____

Friday Date _____	Saturday Date _____

Sunday Date _____	**DAILY SCORECARD**
	1 2 3 4 M ○○○○ T ○○○○ W ○○○○ T ○○○○ F ○○○○ S ○○○○ S ○○○○

Soar

Weekly Task List

Monthly Plan:

Life Duties:

Gratitude

Weekly Assessment

Weekly Achievements:

What problems arose?

What worked well?

What needs adjustment?

Soar

MONTHLY REVIEW for the Month of _____

Social Media Follower Count Growth Tracker:
Facebook   Instagram   Twitter   Website   Pinterest   _____   _____   _____
_____   _____   _____   _____

Sales Tracker:
Income: Salary: Expenses: Profit:

Total Earned (Year-to-Date):

| Completed:

Still in the Works: | Am I closer to my annual goals?

If yes, how will I keep going?

If not, what will I change?

What worked well?

How can I continue? | Obstacles:

What are the causes?

What solutions have I tried?

What else could I try? |

Soar

NOTES AND PLANNING

Soar

Soar

Soar

GOALS for the Month of _____

Work	Health	Self-Care

Creativity	Relationships	Household To-Dos

Soar

Monday	Tuesday	Wednesday	Thursday	Friday	Saturday	Sunday
○	○	○	○	○	○	○
○	○	○	○	○	○	○
○	○	○	○	○	○	○
○	○	○	○	○	○	○
○	○	○	○	○	○	○
○	○	○	○	○	○	○

Habit	1	2	3	4	5	6	7	8	9	10	11	12	13	14	15	16	17	18	19	20	21	22	23	24	25	26	27	28	29	30	31

Soar

MONTHLY BUSINESS PLANNING

TASKS AND TO-DO LIST:

Open:

Closed:

New:

Soar

MONTHLY TASKS TO COMPLETE

WEEK 1	WEEK 2	WEEK 3

WEEK 4	WEEK 5	WEEK 6

Challenges: Rewards: Bonus:

Soar

WEEKLY SPREAD

Monday   Date _____ | Tuesday   Date _____

Wednesday   Date _____ | Thursday   Date _____

Friday   Date _____ | Saturday   Date _____

Sunday   Date _____

DAILY SCORECARD

    1 2 3 4

M ○○○○
T ○○○○
W ○○○○
T ○○○○
F ○○○○
S ○○○○
S ○○○○

Soar

Weekly Task List

Monthly Plan:

Life Duties:

Gratitude

Weekly Assessment

Weekly Achievements:

What problems arose?

What worked well?

What needs adjustment?

Soar

WEEKLY SPREAD

Monday Date _____	Tuesday Date _____

Wednesday Date _____	Thursday Date _____

Friday Date _____	Saturday Date _____

Sunday Date _____	**DAILY SCORECARD**
	1 2 3 4 M ○ ○ ○ ○ T ○ ○ ○ ○ W ○ ○ ○ ○ T ○ ○ ○ ○ F ○ ○ ○ ○ S ○ ○ ○ ○ S ○ ○ ○ ○

Soar

Weekly Task List

Monthly Plan:

Life Duties:

Gratitude

Weekly Assessment

Weekly Achievements:

What problems arose?

What worked well?

What needs adjustment?

Soar

WEEKLY SPREAD

Monday Date _____	Tuesday Date _____

Wednesday Date _____	Thursday Date _____

Friday Date _____	Saturday Date _____

Sunday Date _____	**DAILY SCORECARD**
	1 2 3 4 M ○ ○ ○ ○ T ○ ○ ○ ○ W ○ ○ ○ ○ T ○ ○ ○ ○ F ○ ○ ○ ○ S ○ ○ ○ ○ S ○ ○ ○ ○

Soar

Weekly Task List

Monthly Plan: Life Duties:

Gratitude

Weekly Assessment

Weekly Achievements:	What problems arose?
What worked well?	What needs adjustment?

Soar

WEEKLY SPREAD

Monday Date _____	Tuesday Date _____

Wednesday Date _____	Thursday Date _____

Friday Date _____	Saturday Date _____

Sunday Date _____	**DAILY SCORECARD**
	1 2 3 4 M ○○○○ T ○○○○ W ○○○○ T ○○○○ F ○○○○ S ○○○○ S ○○○○

Soar

Weekly Task List

Monthly Plan:

Life Duties:

Gratitude

Weekly Assessment

Weekly Achievements:	What problems arose?
What worked well?	What needs adjustment?

Soar

WEEKLY SPREAD

Monday Date _____	Tuesday Date _____

Wednesday Date _____	Thursday Date _____

Friday Date _____	Saturday Date _____

Sunday Date _____	**DAILY SCORECARD**
	1 2 3 4 M ○○○○ T ○○○○ W ○○○○ T ○○○○ F ○○○○ S ○○○○ S ○○○○

Soar

Weekly Task List

Monthly Plan: Life Duties:

Gratitude

Weekly Assessment

Weekly Achievements:	What problems arose?
What worked well?	What needs adjustment?

Soar

WEEKLY SPREAD

Monday Date _____	Tuesday Date _____
Wednesday Date _____	Thursday Date _____
Friday Date _____	Saturday Date _____
Sunday Date _____	**DAILY SCORECARD**

DAILY SCORECARD

    1 2 3 4
M ○ ○ ○ ○
T ○ ○ ○ ○
W ○ ○ ○ ○
T ○ ○ ○ ○
F ○ ○ ○ ○
S ○ ○ ○ ○
S ○ ○ ○ ○

Soar

WEEKLY TASK LIST

Monthly Plan: Life Duties:

Gratitude

WEEKLY ASSESSMENT

Weekly Achievements:	What problems arose?
What worked well?	What needs adjustment?

MONTHLY REVIEW for the Month of _____

Social Media Follower Count Growth Tracker:
Facebook   Instagram   Twitter   Website   Pinterest   ____   ____   ____
____   ____   ____   ____   ____   ____   ____

Sales Tracker:
Income: Salary: Expenses: Profit:

Total Earned (Year-to-Date):

Completed:	Am I closer to my annual goals? If yes, how will I keep going? If not, what will I change?	Obstacles: What are the causes? What solutions have I tried? What else could I try?
Still in the Works:		
	What worked well? How can I continue?	

Notes and Planning

Soar

Soar

Soar

Soar

GOALS for the Month of _____

Work	Health	Self-Care

Creativity	Relationships	Household To-Dos

Soar

Monday	Tuesday	Wednesday	Thursday	Friday	Saturday	Sunday
○	○	○	○	○	○	○
○	○	○	○	○	○	○
○	○	○	○	○	○	○
○	○	○	○	○	○	○
○	○	○	○	○	○	○
○	○	○	○	○	○	○

Habit	1	2	3	4	5	6	7	8	9	10	11	12	13	14	15	16	17	18	19	20	21	22	23	24	25	26	27	28	29	30	31

Soar

Monthly Business Planning

Tasks and To-Do List:

Open:

Closed:

New:

Soar

MONTHLY TASKS TO COMPLETE

WEEK 1	WEEK 2	WEEK 3

WEEK 4	WEEK 5	WEEK 6

Challenges: Rewards: Bonus:

Soar

WEEKLY SPREAD

Monday Date _____	Tuesday Date _____
Wednesday Date _____	Thursday Date _____
Friday Date _____	Saturday Date _____
Sunday Date _____	**DAILY SCORECARD** 1 2 3 4 M ○○○○ T ○○○○ W ○○○○ T ○○○○ F ○○○○ S ○○○○ S ○○○○

Soar

Weekly Task List

Monthly Plan: Life Duties:

Gratitude

Weekly Assessment

Weekly Achievements:	What problems arose?
What worked well?	What needs adjustment?

Soar

WEEKLY SPREAD

Monday Date _____	Tuesday Date _____

Wednesday Date _____	Thursday Date _____

Friday Date _____	Saturday Date _____

Sunday Date _____	**DAILY SCORECARD**
	1 2 3 4 M ○ ○ ○ ○ T ○ ○ ○ ○ W ○ ○ ○ ○ T ○ ○ ○ ○ F ○ ○ ○ ○ S ○ ○ ○ ○ S ○ ○ ○ ○

Soar

Weekly Task List

Monthly Plan:

Life Duties:

Gratitude

Weekly Assessment

Weekly Achievements:	What problems arose?
What worked well?	What needs adjustment?

Soar

WEEKLY SPREAD

Monday Date _____	Tuesday Date _____

Wednesday Date _____	Thursday Date _____

Friday Date _____	Saturday Date _____

Sunday Date _____	**DAILY SCORECARD**
	1 2 3 4 M ○○○○ T ○○○○ W ○○○○ T ○○○○ F ○○○○ S ○○○○ S ○○○○

Soar

WEEKLY TASK LIST

Monthly Plan: Life Duties:

Gratitude

WEEKLY ASSESSMENT

Weekly Achievements:	What problems arose?
What worked well?	What needs adjustment?

Soar

WEEKLY SPREAD

Monday Date _____	Tuesday Date _____

Wednesday Date _____	Thursday Date _____

Friday Date _____	Saturday Date _____

Sunday Date _____	**DAILY SCORECARD**
	1 2 3 4 M ○ ○ ○ ○ T ○ ○ ○ ○ W ○ ○ ○ ○ T ○ ○ ○ ○ F ○ ○ ○ ○ S ○ ○ ○ ○ S ○ ○ ○ ○

Soar

WEEKLY TASK LIST

Monthly Plan: Life Duties:

Gratitude

WEEKLY ASSESSMENT

Weekly Achievements:	What problems arose?
What worked well?	What needs adjustment?

Soar

WEEKLY SPREAD

Monday Date _____	Tuesday Date _____
Wednesday Date _____	Thursday Date _____
Friday Date _____	Saturday Date _____
Sunday Date _____	**DAILY SCORECARD** 　　　1 2 3 4 M ○ ○ ○ ○ T ○ ○ ○ ○ W ○ ○ ○ ○ T ○ ○ ○ ○ F ○ ○ ○ ○ S ○ ○ ○ ○ S ○ ○ ○ ○

Soar

Weekly Task List

Monthly Plan: Life Duties:

Gratitude

Weekly Assessment

Weekly Achievements:	What problems arose?
What worked well?	What needs adjustment?

Soar

WEEKLY SPREAD

Monday Date _____	Tuesday Date _____
Wednesday Date _____	Thursday Date _____
Friday Date _____	Saturday Date _____
Sunday Date _____	**DAILY SCORECARD**

Daily Scorecard:

```
      1 2 3 4
  M   O O O O
  T   O O O O
  W   O O O O
  T   O O O O
  F   O O O O
  S   O O O O
  S   O O O O
```

Soar

WEEKLY TASK LIST

Monthly Plan: Life Duties:

Gratitude

WEEKLY ASSESSMENT

Weekly Achievements:	What problems arose?
What worked well?	What needs adjustment?

MONTHLY REVIEW for the Month of _____

Social Media Follower Count Growth Tracker:
Facebook   Instagram   Twitter   Website   Pinterest   _____   _____   _____
_____   _____   _____   _____   _____   _____   _____   _____

Sales Tracker:
Income: Salary: Expenses: Profit:

Total Earned (Year-to-Date):

Completed:	Am I closer to my annual goals?	Obstacles:
	If yes, how will I keep going?	
		What are the causes?
	If not, what will I change?	
Still in the Works:		What solutions have I tried?
	What worked well?	
		What else could I try?
	How can I continue?	

152

Soar

NOTES AND PLANNING

Soar

Soar

Soar

QUARTERLY RAPID LOG:

QUARTERLY PROGRESS LOG

Writing	Editing/Proofreading
Social Media	Graphics
Public Speaking/Publicity	Web Design
Marketing	Advertising
Bookkeeping	Professional Organizations
Continuing Education	Podcasting
Blogging	Sales

Soar

GOALS for the Month of _____

Work	Health	Self-Care
Creativity	Relationships	Household To-Dos

Soar

Monday	Tuesday	Wednesday	Thursday	Friday	Saturday	Sunday
○	○	○	○	○	○	○
○	○	○	○	○	○	○
○	○	○	○	○	○	○
○	○	○	○	○	○	○
○	○	○	○	○	○	○
○	○	○	○	○	○	○

Habit	1	2	3	4	5	6	7	8	9	10	11	12	13	14	15	16	17	18	19	20	21	22	23	24	25	26	27	28	29	30	31

Soar

Monthly Business Planning

Tasks and To-Do List:

Open:

Closed:

New:

Soar

MONTHLY TASKS TO COMPLETE

Week 1	Week 2	Week 3

Week 4	Week 5	Week 6

Challenges: Rewards: Bonus:

Soar

WEEKLY SPREAD

Monday Date _____	Tuesday Date _____
Wednesday Date _____	Thursday Date _____
Friday Date _____	Saturday Date _____
Sunday Date _____	**DAILY SCORECARD**

Daily Scorecard:

```
        1 2 3 4
    M   O O O O
    T   O O O O
    W   O O O O
    T   O O O O
    F   O O O O
    S   O O O O
    S   O O O O
```

Soar

WEEKLY TASK LIST

Monthly Plan: Life Duties:

Gratitude

WEEKLY ASSESSMENT

Weekly Achievements:	What problems arose?
What worked well?	What needs adjustment?

Soar

WEEKLY SPREAD

Monday Date _____	Tuesday Date _____

Wednesday Date _____	Thursday Date _____

Friday Date _____	Saturday Date _____

Sunday Date _____	**DAILY SCORECARD**
	1 2 3 4 M ○ ○ ○ ○ T ○ ○ ○ ○ W ○ ○ ○ ○ T ○ ○ ○ ○ F ○ ○ ○ ○ S ○ ○ ○ ○ S ○ ○ ○ ○

Soar

Weekly Task List

Monthly Plan:

Life Duties:

Gratitude

Weekly Assessment

Weekly Achievements:

What problems arose?

What worked well?

What needs adjustment?

Soar

WEEKLY SPREAD

Monday Date _____	Tuesday Date _____

Wednesday Date _____	Thursday Date _____

Friday Date _____	Saturday Date _____

Sunday Date _____	**DAILY SCORECARD**
	1 2 3 4 M ○○○○ T ○○○○ W ○○○○ T ○○○○ F ○○○○ S ○○○○ S ○○○○

Soar

Weekly Task List

Monthly Plan:

Life Duties:

Gratitude

Weekly Assessment

Weekly Achievements:	What problems arose?
What worked well?	What needs adjustment?

Soar

WEEKLY SPREAD

Monday Date _____	Tuesday Date _____

Wednesday Date _____	Thursday Date _____

Friday Date _____	Saturday Date _____

Sunday Date _____	**DAILY SCORECARD**
	1 2 3 4 M ○ ○ ○ ○ T ○ ○ ○ ○ W ○ ○ ○ ○ T ○ ○ ○ ○ F ○ ○ ○ ○ S ○ ○ ○ ○ S ○ ○ ○ ○

Soar

Weekly Task List

Monthly Plan:

Life Duties:

Gratitude

Weekly Assessment

Weekly Achievements:	What problems arose?
What worked well?	What needs adjustment?

Soar

WEEKLY SPREAD

Monday Date _____	Tuesday Date _____
Wednesday Date _____	Thursday Date _____
Friday Date _____	Saturday Date _____
Sunday Date _____	**DAILY SCORECARD**

DAILY SCORECARD

    1 2 3 4
M ○○○○
T ○○○○
W ○○○○
T ○○○○
F ○○○○
S ○○○○
S ○○○○

Soar

Weekly Task List

Monthly Plan:

Life Duties:

Gratitude

Weekly Assessment

Weekly Achievements:

What problems arose?

What worked well?

What needs adjustment?

Soar

WEEKLY SPREAD

Monday Date _____	Tuesday Date _____
Wednesday Date _____	**Thursday** Date _____
Friday Date _____	**Saturday** Date _____
Sunday Date _____	**DAILY SCORECARD**

DAILY SCORECARD

```
      1 2 3 4
  M  ○ ○ ○ ○
  T  ○ ○ ○ ○
  W  ○ ○ ○ ○
  T  ○ ○ ○ ○
  F  ○ ○ ○ ○
  S  ○ ○ ○ ○
  S  ○ ○ ○ ○
```

Soar

Weekly Task List

Monthly Plan: Life Duties:

Gratitude

Weekly Assessment

Weekly Achievements:	What problems arose?
What worked well?	What needs adjustment?

Soar

MONTHLY REVIEW for the Month of _____

Social Media Follower Count Growth Tracker:
Facebook   Instagram   Twitter   Website   Pinterest   _____   _____   _____
_____   _____   _____   _____   _____   _____   _____

Sales Tracker:
Income: Salary: Expenses: Profit:

Total Earned (Year-to-Date):

Completed:	Am I closer to my annual goals?	Obstacles:
	If yes, how will I keep going?	
		What are the causes?
	If not, what will I change?	
Still in the Works:		What solutions have I tried?
	What worked well?	
		What else could I try?
	How can I continue?	

NOTES AND PLANNING

Soar

Soar

Soar

Soar

GOALS for the Month of _____

Work	Health	Self-Care

Creativity	Relationships	Household To-Dos

Soar

Monday	Tuesday	Wednesday	Thursday	Friday	Saturday	Sunday
○	○	○	○	○	○	○
○	○	○	○	○	○	○
○	○	○	○	○	○	○
○	○	○	○	○	○	○
○	○	○	○	○	○	○
○	○	○	○	○	○	○

Habit	1	2	3	4	5	6	7	8	9	10	11	12	13	14	15	16	17	18	19	20	21	22	23	24	25	26	27	28	29	30	31

Soar

MONTHLY BUSINESS PLANNING

TASKS AND TO-DO LIST:

Open:

Closed:

New:

Soar

Monthly Tasks to Complete

Week 1	Week 2	Week 3

Week 4	Week 5	Week 6

Challenges: Rewards: Bonus:

Soar

WEEKLY SPREAD

Monday Date _____	Tuesday Date _____
Wednesday Date _____	Thursday Date _____
Friday Date _____	Saturday Date _____
Sunday Date _____	**DAILY SCORECARD**

Daily Scorecard

```
      1 2 3 4
   M  ○ ○ ○ ○
   T  ○ ○ ○ ○
   W  ○ ○ ○ ○
   T  ○ ○ ○ ○
   F  ○ ○ ○ ○
   S  ○ ○ ○ ○
   S  ○ ○ ○ ○
```

Soar

Weekly Task List

Monthly Plan: Life Duties:

Gratitude

Weekly Assessment

Weekly Achievements:	What problems arose?
What worked well?	What needs adjustment?

Soar

WEEKLY SPREAD

Monday Date _____	Tuesday Date _____

Wednesday Date _____	Thursday Date _____

Friday Date _____	Saturday Date _____

Sunday Date _____	**DAILY SCORECARD**
	1 2 3 4 M ○ ○ ○ ○ T ○ ○ ○ ○ W ○ ○ ○ ○ T ○ ○ ○ ○ F ○ ○ ○ ○ S ○ ○ ○ ○ S ○ ○ ○ ○

Soar

Weekly Task List

Monthly Plan:

Life Duties:

Gratitude

Weekly Assessment

Weekly Achievements:

What problems arose?

What worked well?

What needs adjustment?

Soar

WEEKLY SPREAD

Monday Date _____	Tuesday Date _____

Wednesday Date _____	Thursday Date _____

Friday Date _____	Saturday Date _____

Sunday Date _____	**DAILY SCORECARD**
	1 2 3 4 M ○○○○ T ○○○○ W ○○○○ T ○○○○ F ○○○○ S ○○○○ S ○○○○

Soar

Weekly Task List

Monthly Plan: Life Duties:

Gratitude

Weekly Assessment

Weekly Achievements:	What problems arose?
What worked well?	What needs adjustment?

Soar

WEEKLY SPREAD

Monday Date _____	Tuesday Date _____
Wednesday Date _____	Thursday Date _____
Friday Date _____	Saturday Date _____
Sunday Date _____	**DAILY SCORECARD**

DAILY SCORECARD

    1 2 3 4
M ○○○○
T ○○○○
W ○○○○
T ○○○○
F ○○○○
S ○○○○
S ○○○○

Soar

WEEKLY TASK LIST

Monthly Plan:

Life Duties:

Gratitude

WEEKLY ASSESSMENT

Weekly Achievements:

What problems arose?

What worked well?

What needs adjustment?

Soar

WEEKLY SPREAD

Monday Date _____	Tuesday Date _____

Wednesday Date _____	Thursday Date _____

Friday Date _____	Saturday Date _____

Sunday Date _____	**DAILY SCORECARD**
	1 2 3 4 M ○○○○ T ○○○○ W ○○○○ T ○○○○ F ○○○○ S ○○○○ S ○○○○

Soar

Weekly Task List

Monthly Plan:

Life Duties:

Gratitude

Weekly Assessment

Weekly Achievements:	What problems arose?
What worked well?	What needs adjustment?

Soar

WEEKLY SPREAD

Monday Date _____	Tuesday Date _____

Wednesday Date _____	Thursday Date _____

Friday Date _____	Saturday Date _____

Sunday Date _____	**DAILY SCORECARD**
	1 2 3 4 M ○○○○ T ○○○○ W ○○○○ T ○○○○ F ○○○○ S ○○○○ S ○○○○

Soar

Weekly Task List

Monthly Plan: Life Duties:

Gratitude

Weekly Assessment

Weekly Achievements:	What problems arose?
What worked well?	What needs adjustment?

MONTHLY REVIEW for the Month of _____

Social Media Follower Count Growth Tracker:
Facebook   Instagram   Twitter   Website   Pinterest   _____   _____   _____
_____   _____   _____   _____   _____   _____   _____   _____

Sales Tracker:
Income: Salary: Expenses: Profit:

Total Earned (Year-to-Date):

Completed:	Am I closer to my annual goals?	Obstacles:
	If yes, how will I keep going?	
		What are the causes?
	If not, what will I change?	
Still in the Works:		What solutions have I tried?
	What worked well?	
		What else could I try?
	How can I continue?	

Notes and Planning

Soar

Soar

Soar

Soar

GOALS for the Month of _____

Work	Health	Self-Care

Creativity	Relationships	Household To-Dos

Soar

Monday	Tuesday	Wednesday	Thursday	Friday	Saturday	Sunday
○	○	○	○	○	○	○
○	○	○	○	○	○	○
○	○	○	○	○	○	○
○	○	○	○	○	○	○
○	○	○	○	○	○	○
○	○	○	○	○	○	○

Habit	1	2	3	4	5	6	7	8	9	10	11	12	13	14	15	16	17	18	19	20	21	22	23	24	25	26	27	28	29	30	31

Soar

Monthly Business Planning

Tasks and To-Do List:

Open:

Closed:

New:

Soar

MONTHLY TASKS TO COMPLETE

WEEK 1	WEEK 2	WEEK 3
WEEK 4	**WEEK 5**	**WEEK 6**

Challenges: Rewards: Bonus:

Soar

WEEKLY SPREAD

Monday Date _____	Tuesday Date _____
Wednesday Date _____	Thursday Date _____
Friday Date _____	Saturday Date _____
Sunday Date _____	**DAILY SCORECARD**
	1 2 3 4 M ○ ○ ○ ○ T ○ ○ ○ ○ W ○ ○ ○ ○ T ○ ○ ○ ○ F ○ ○ ○ ○ S ○ ○ ○ ○ S ○ ○ ○ ○

Soar

Weekly Task List

Monthly Plan:

Life Duties:

Gratitude

Weekly Assessment

Weekly Achievements:

What problems arose?

What worked well?

What needs adjustment?

Soar

WEEKLY SPREAD

Monday Date _____	Tuesday Date _____

Wednesday Date _____	Thursday Date _____

Friday Date _____	Saturday Date _____

Sunday Date _____	**DAILY SCORECARD**
	1 2 3 4 M ○ ○ ○ ○ T ○ ○ ○ ○ W ○ ○ ○ ○ T ○ ○ ○ ○ F ○ ○ ○ ○ S ○ ○ ○ ○ S ○ ○ ○ ○

Soar

Weekly Task List

Monthly Plan:

Life Duties:

Gratitude

Weekly Assessment

Weekly Achievements:	What problems arose?
What worked well?	What needs adjustment?

Soar

WEEKLY SPREAD

Monday Date _____	Tuesday Date _____

Wednesday Date _____	Thursday Date _____

Friday Date _____	Saturday Date _____

Sunday Date _____	**DAILY SCORECARD**
	1 2 3 4 M ○ ○ ○ ○ T ○ ○ ○ ○ W ○ ○ ○ ○ T ○ ○ ○ ○ F ○ ○ ○ ○ S ○ ○ ○ ○ S ○ ○ ○ ○

Soar

Weekly Task List

Monthly Plan:

Life Duties:

Gratitude

Weekly Assessment

Weekly Achievements:	What problems arose?
What worked well?	What needs adjustment?

Soar

WEEKLY SPREAD

Monday Date _____	Tuesday Date _____
Wednesday Date _____	Thursday Date _____
Friday Date _____	Saturday Date _____
Sunday Date _____	**DAILY SCORECARD**

DAILY SCORECARD

    1 2 3 4
M ○ ○ ○ ○
T ○ ○ ○ ○
W ○ ○ ○ ○
T ○ ○ ○ ○
F ○ ○ ○ ○
S ○ ○ ○ ○
S ○ ○ ○ ○

Soar

Weekly Task List

Monthly Plan:

Life Duties:

Gratitude

Weekly Assessment

Weekly Achievements:

What problems arose?

What worked well?

What needs adjustment?

Soar

WEEKLY SPREAD

Monday Date _____	Tuesday Date _____
Wednesday Date _____	Thursday Date _____
Friday Date _____	Saturday Date _____
Sunday Date _____	**DAILY SCORECARD**

        1 2 3 4
M ○ ○ ○ ○
T ○ ○ ○ ○
W ○ ○ ○ ○
T ○ ○ ○ ○
F ○ ○ ○ ○
S ○ ○ ○ ○
S ○ ○ ○ ○

Soar

Weekly Task List

Monthly Plan:

Life Duties:

Gratitude

Weekly Assessment

Weekly Achievements:	What problems arose?
What worked well?	What needs adjustment?

Soar

WEEKLY SPREAD

Monday Date _____	Tuesday Date _____
Wednesday Date _____	Thursday Date _____
Friday Date _____	Saturday Date _____
Sunday Date _____	**DAILY SCORECARD**

```
       1 2 3 4
    M  O O O O
    T  O O O O
    W  O O O O
    T  O O O O
    F  O O O O
    S  O O O O
    S  O O O O
```

Soar

WEEKLY TASK LIST

Monthly Plan:

Life Duties:

Gratitude

WEEKLY ASSESSMENT

Weekly Achievements:	What problems arose?
What worked well?	What needs adjustment?

Soar

MONTHLY REVIEW for the Month of _____

Social Media Follower Count Growth Tracker:
Facebook   Instagram   Twitter   Website   Pinterest   _____   _____   _____
_____   _____   _____   _____   _____   _____   _____

Sales Tracker:
Income: Salary: Expenses: Profit:

Total Earned (Year-to-Date):

Completed:	Am I closer to my annual goals?	Obstacles:
	If yes, how will I keep going?	
		What are the causes?
	If not, what will I change?	
Still in the Works:		What solutions have I tried?
	What worked well?	
		What else could I try?
	How can I continue?	

Soar

NOTES AND PLANNING

Soar

Soar

Soar

QUARTERLY RAPID LOG:

Soar

QUARTERLY PROGRESS LOG

Writing	Editing/Proofreading
Social Media	Graphics
Public Speaking/Publicity	Web Design
Marketing	Advertising
Bookkeeping	Professional Organizations
Continuing Education	Podcasting
Blogging	Sales

Soar

GOALS for the Month of _____

Work	Health	Self-Care

Creativity	Relationships	Household To-Dos

Soar

Monday	Tuesday	Wednesday	Thursday	Friday	Saturday	Sunday
○	○	○	○	○	○	○
○	○	○	○	○	○	○
○	○	○	○	○	○	○
○	○	○	○	○	○	○
○	○	○	○	○	○	○
○	○	○	○	○	○	○

Habit	1	2	3	4	5	6	7	8	9	10	11	12	13	14	15	16	17	18	19	20	21	22	23	24	25	26	27	28	29	30	31

Soar

Monthly Business Planning

Tasks and To-Do List:

Open:

Closed:

New:

Soar

MONTHLY TASKS TO COMPLETE

WEEK 1	WEEK 2	WEEK 3

WEEK 4	WEEK 5	WEEK 6

Challenges: Rewards: Bonus:

Soar

WEEKLY SPREAD

Monday Date _____	Tuesday Date _____

Wednesday Date _____	Thursday Date _____

Friday Date _____	Saturday Date _____

Sunday Date _____	**DAILY SCORECARD**
	1 2 3 4 M ○○○○ T ○○○○ W ○○○○ T ○○○○ F ○○○○ S ○○○○ S ○○○○

Soar

Weekly Task List

Monthly Plan:

Life Duties:

Gratitude

Weekly Assessment

Weekly Achievements:

What problems arose?

What worked well?

What needs adjustment?

Soar

WEEKLY SPREAD

Monday Date _____	Tuesday Date _____

Wednesday Date _____	Thursday Date _____

Friday Date _____	Saturday Date _____

Sunday Date _____	**DAILY SCORECARD**
	1 2 3 4 M ○ ○ ○ ○ T ○ ○ ○ ○ W ○ ○ ○ ○ T ○ ○ ○ ○ F ○ ○ ○ ○ S ○ ○ ○ ○ S ○ ○ ○ ○

Soar

WEEKLY TASK LIST

Monthly Plan: Life Duties:

Gratitude

WEEKLY ASSESSMENT

Weekly Achievements:	What problems arose?
What worked well?	What needs adjustment?

Soar

WEEKLY SPREAD

Monday Date _____	Tuesday Date _____
Wednesday Date _____	Thursday Date _____
Friday Date _____	Saturday Date _____
Sunday Date _____	**DAILY SCORECARD**

Daily Scorecard

    1 2 3 4
M ○○○○
T ○○○○
W ○○○○
T ○○○○
F ○○○○
S ○○○○
S ○○○○

Soar

WEEKLY TASK LIST

Monthly Plan: Life Duties:

Gratitude

WEEKLY ASSESSMENT

Weekly Achievements:	What problems arose?
What worked well?	What needs adjustment?

Soar

WEEKLY SPREAD

Monday Date _____	Tuesday Date _____
Wednesday Date _____	Thursday Date _____
Friday Date _____	Saturday Date _____
Sunday Date _____	**DAILY SCORECARD**

DAILY SCORECARD

    1 2 3 4
M ○○○○
T ○○○○
W ○○○○
T ○○○○
F ○○○○
S ○○○○
S ○○○○

Soar

WEEKLY TASK LIST

Monthly Plan: Life Duties:

Gratitude

WEEKLY ASSESSMENT

Weekly Achievements:	What problems arose?
What worked well?	What needs adjustment?

Soar

WEEKLY SPREAD

Monday Date _____	Tuesday Date _____
Wednesday Date _____	Thursday Date _____
Friday Date _____	Saturday Date _____
Sunday Date _____	**DAILY SCORECARD**

Daily Scorecard:

```
    1 2 3 4
M  ○ ○ ○ ○
T  ○ ○ ○ ○
W  ○ ○ ○ ○
T  ○ ○ ○ ○
F  ○ ○ ○ ○
S  ○ ○ ○ ○
S  ○ ○ ○ ○
```

Soar

Weekly Task List

Monthly Plan:

Life Duties:

Gratitude

Weekly Assessment

Weekly Achievements:

What problems arose?

What worked well?

What needs adjustment?

Soar

WEEKLY SPREAD

Monday Date _____	Tuesday Date _____
Wednesday Date _____	Thursday Date _____
Friday Date _____	Saturday Date _____
Sunday Date _____	**DAILY SCORECARD**

DAILY SCORECARD

	1	2	3	4
M	○	○	○	○
T	○	○	○	○
W	○	○	○	○
T	○	○	○	○
F	○	○	○	○
S	○	○	○	○
S	○	○	○	○

Soar

WEEKLY TASK LIST

Monthly Plan:

Life Duties:

Gratitude

WEEKLY ASSESSMENT

Weekly Achievements:

What problems arose?

What worked well?

What needs adjustment?

Soar

MONTHLY REVIEW for the Month of _____

Social Media Follower Count Growth Tracker:
Facebook   Instagram   Twitter   Website   Pinterest   _____   _____   _____

_____   _____   _____   _____   _____   _____   _____   _____

Sales Tracker:
Income: Salary: Expenses: Profit:

Total Earned (Year-to-Date):

Completed:	Am I closer to my annual goals?	Obstacles:
	If yes, how will I keep going?	
		What are the causes?
	If not, what will I change?	
Still in the Works:		What solutions have I tried?
	What worked well?	
		What else could I try?
	How can I continue?	

Notes and Planning

Soar

Soar

Soar

GOALS for the Month of _____

Work	Health	Self-Care

Creativity	Relationships	Household To-Dos

Soar

Monday	Tuesday	Wednesday	Thursday	Friday	Saturday	Sunday
○	○	○	○	○	○	○
○	○	○	○	○	○	○
○	○	○	○	○	○	○
○	○	○	○	○	○	○
○	○	○	○	○	○	○
○	○	○	○	○	○	○

Habit	1	2	3	4	5	6	7	8	9	10	11	12	13	14	15	16	17	18	19	20	21	22	23	24	25	26	27	28	29	30	31

Soar

MONTHLY BUSINESS PLANNING

TASKS AND TO-DO LIST:

Open:

Closed:

New:

Soar

MONTHLY TASKS TO COMPLETE

Week 1	Week 2	Week 3

Week 4	Week 5	Week 6

Challenges:	Rewards:	Bonus:

Soar

WEEKLY SPREAD

Monday Date _____	Tuesday Date _____
Wednesday Date _____	Thursday Date _____
Friday Date _____	Saturday Date _____
Sunday Date _____	**DAILY SCORECARD** 　　　　1 2 3 4 M ○ ○ ○ ○ T ○ ○ ○ ○ W ○ ○ ○ ○ T ○ ○ ○ ○ F ○ ○ ○ ○ S ○ ○ ○ ○ S ○ ○ ○ ○

Soar

Weekly Task List

Monthly Plan:　　　　　　　　　Life Duties:

Gratitude

Weekly Assessment

Weekly Achievements:	What problems arose?
What worked well?	What needs adjustment?

Soar

WEEKLY SPREAD

Monday Date _____	Tuesday Date _____
Wednesday Date _____	Thursday Date _____
Friday Date _____	Saturday Date _____
Sunday Date _____	**DAILY SCORECARD**

Daily Scorecard:

```
      1 2 3 4
  M  ○ ○ ○ ○
  T  ○ ○ ○ ○
  W  ○ ○ ○ ○
  T  ○ ○ ○ ○
  F  ○ ○ ○ ○
  S  ○ ○ ○ ○
  S  ○ ○ ○ ○
```

Soar

Weekly Task List

Monthly Plan:

Life Duties:

Gratitude

Weekly Assessment

Weekly Achievements:	What problems arose?
What worked well?	What needs adjustment?

Soar

WEEKLY SPREAD

Monday Date _____	Tuesday Date _____
Wednesday Date _____	Thursday Date _____
Friday Date _____	Saturday Date _____
Sunday Date _____	**DAILY SCORECARD**

DAILY SCORECARD

    1 2 3 4
M ○ ○ ○ ○
T ○ ○ ○ ○
W ○ ○ ○ ○
T ○ ○ ○ ○
F ○ ○ ○ ○
S ○ ○ ○ ○
S ○ ○ ○ ○

Soar

WEEKLY TASK LIST

Monthly Plan:

Life Duties:

Gratitude

WEEKLY ASSESSMENT

Weekly Achievements:

What problems arose?

What worked well?

What needs adjustment?

Soar

WEEKLY SPREAD

Monday Date _____	Tuesday Date _____
Wednesday Date _____	Thursday Date _____
Friday Date _____	Saturday Date _____
Sunday Date _____	**DAILY SCORECARD** 1 2 3 4 M ○ ○ ○ ○ T ○ ○ ○ ○ W ○ ○ ○ ○ T ○ ○ ○ ○ F ○ ○ ○ ○ S ○ ○ ○ ○ S ○ ○ ○ ○

Soar

Weekly Task List

Monthly Plan:

Life Duties:

Gratitude

Weekly Assessment

Weekly Achievements:	What problems arose?
What worked well?	What needs adjustment?

Soar

WEEKLY SPREAD

Monday Date _____	Tuesday Date _____

Wednesday Date _____	Thursday Date _____

Friday Date _____	Saturday Date _____

Sunday Date _____	**DAILY SCORECARD**
	1 2 3 4 M ○ ○ ○ ○ T ○ ○ ○ ○ W ○ ○ ○ ○ T ○ ○ ○ ○ F ○ ○ ○ ○ S ○ ○ ○ ○ S ○ ○ ○ ○

Soar

WEEKLY TASK LIST

Monthly Plan:

Life Duties:

Gratitude

WEEKLY ASSESSMENT

Weekly Achievements:

What problems arose?

What worked well?

What needs adjustment?

Soar

WEEKLY SPREAD

Monday Date _____	Tuesday Date _____

Wednesday Date _____	Thursday Date _____

Friday Date _____	Saturday Date _____

Sunday Date _____	**DAILY SCORECARD**
	1 2 3 4 M ○ ○ ○ ○ T ○ ○ ○ ○ W ○ ○ ○ ○ T ○ ○ ○ ○ F ○ ○ ○ ○ S ○ ○ ○ ○ S ○ ○ ○ ○

Soar

WEEKLY TASK LIST

Monthly Plan:					Life Duties:

Gratitude

WEEKLY ASSESSMENT

Weekly Achievements:	What problems arose?
What worked well?	What needs adjustment?

Soar

MONTHLY REVIEW for the Month of _____

Social Media Follower Count Growth Tracker:
Facebook   Instagram   Twitter   Website   Pinterest   _____   _____   _____
_____   _____   _____   _____   _____   _____   _____

Sales Tracker:
Income: Salary: Expenses: Profit:

Total Earned (Year-to-Date):

Completed:	Am I closer to my annual goals?	Obstacles:
	If yes, how will I keep going?	What are the causes?
	If not, what will I change?	What solutions have I tried?
Still in the Works:		
	What worked well?	What else could I try?
	How can I continue?	

Soar

NOTES AND PLANNING

Soar

Soar

Soar

GOALS for the Month of _____

Work	Health	Self-Care

Creativity	Relationships	Household To-Dos

Soar

Monday	Tuesday	Wednesday	Thursday	Friday	Saturday	Sunday
○	○	○	○	○	○	○
○	○	○	○	○	○	○
○	○	○	○	○	○	○
○	○	○	○	○	○	○
○	○	○	○	○	○	○
○	○	○	○	○	○	○

Habit	1	2	3	4	5	6	7	8	9	10	11	12	13	14	15	16	17	18	19	20	21	22	23	24	25	26	27	28	29	30	31

Soar
Monthly Business Planning

Tasks and To-Do List:

Open:

Closed:

New:

Soar

MONTHLY TASKS TO COMPLETE

Week 1	Week 2	Week 3

Week 4	Week 5	Week 6

Challenges: Rewards: Bonus:

Soar

WEEKLY SPREAD

Monday Date _____	Tuesday Date _____

Wednesday Date _____	Thursday Date _____

Friday Date _____	Saturday Date _____

Sunday Date _____	**DAILY SCORECARD**
	1 2 3 4 M ○ ○ ○ ○ T ○ ○ ○ ○ W ○ ○ ○ ○ T ○ ○ ○ ○ F ○ ○ ○ ○ S ○ ○ ○ ○ S ○ ○ ○ ○

Soar

WEEKLY TASK LIST

Monthly Plan:

Life Duties:

Gratitude

WEEKLY ASSESSMENT

Weekly Achievements:	What problems arose?
What worked well?	What needs adjustment?

Soar

WEEKLY SPREAD

Monday Date _____	Tuesday Date _____

Wednesday Date _____	Thursday Date _____

Friday Date _____	Saturday Date _____

Sunday Date _____	**DAILY SCORECARD**
	1 2 3 4 M ○ ○ ○ ○ T ○ ○ ○ ○ W ○ ○ ○ ○ T ○ ○ ○ ○ F ○ ○ ○ ○ S ○ ○ ○ ○ S ○ ○ ○ ○

Soar

Weekly Task List

Monthly Plan: Life Duties:

Gratitude

Weekly Assessment

Weekly Achievements: What problems arose?

What worked well?   What needs adjustment?

Soar

WEEKLY SPREAD

Monday Date _____	Tuesday Date _____

Wednesday Date _____	Thursday Date _____

Friday Date _____	Saturday Date _____

Sunday Date _____	**DAILY SCORECARD**
	1 2 3 4 M ○○○○ T ○○○○ W ○○○○ T ○○○○ F ○○○○ S ○○○○ S ○○○○

Soar

WEEKLY TASK LIST

Monthly Plan: Life Duties:

Gratitude

WEEKLY ASSESSMENT

Weekly Achievements: What problems arose?

What worked well?   What needs adjustment?

Soar

WEEKLY SPREAD

Monday Date _____	Tuesday Date _____

Wednesday Date _____	Thursday Date _____

Friday Date _____	Saturday Date _____

Sunday Date _____	**DAILY SCORECARD**
	1 2 3 4 M ○ ○ ○ ○ T ○ ○ ○ ○ W ○ ○ ○ ○ T ○ ○ ○ ○ F ○ ○ ○ ○ S ○ ○ ○ ○ S ○ ○ ○ ○

Soar

Weekly Task List

Monthly Plan:

Life Duties:

Gratitude

Weekly Assessment

Weekly Achievements:

What problems arose?

What worked well?

What needs adjustment?

Soar

WEEKLY SPREAD

Monday Date _____	Tuesday Date _____

Wednesday Date _____	Thursday Date _____

Friday Date _____	Saturday Date _____

Sunday Date _____	**DAILY SCORECARD**
	1 2 3 4 M ○ ○ ○ ○ T ○ ○ ○ ○ W ○ ○ ○ ○ T ○ ○ ○ ○ F ○ ○ ○ ○ S ○ ○ ○ ○ S ○ ○ ○ ○

Soar

WEEKLY TASK LIST

Monthly Plan:

Life Duties:

Gratitude

WEEKLY ASSESSMENT

Weekly Achievements:

What problems arose?

What worked well?

What needs adjustment?

Soar

WEEKLY SPREAD

Monday Date _____	Tuesday Date _____
Wednesday Date _____	Thursday Date _____
Friday Date _____	Saturday Date _____
Sunday Date _____	**DAILY SCORECARD**
	1 2 3 4 M ○○○○ T ○○○○ W ○○○○ T ○○○○ F ○○○○ S ○○○○ S ○○○○

Soar

WEEKLY TASK LIST

Monthly Plan:					Life Duties:

Gratitude

WEEKLY ASSESSMENT

Weekly Achievements:	What problems arose?
What worked well?	What needs adjustment?

Soar

MONTHLY REVIEW for the Month of _____

Social Media Follower Count Growth Tracker:
Facebook   Instagram   Twitter   Website   Pinterest   _____   _____   _____
_____   _____   _____   _____   _____   _____   _____

Sales Tracker:
Income: Salary: Expenses: Profit:

Total Earned (Year-to-Date):

Completed:	Am I closer to my annual goals?	Obstacles:
	If yes, how will I keep going?	
		What are the causes?
	If not, what will I change?	
Still in the Works:		What solutions have I tried?
	What worked well?	
		What else could I try?
	How can I continue?	

Notes and Planning

Soar

Soar

ANNUAL REVIEW

You made it!
Time to do some reflection and self-assessment so you can plan for the future.

Maybe this year went exactly like you planned, but if you're like me, you'll realize that you've got some goals that need revision. Even if you didn't accomplish everything you set out for yourself a year ago, that doesn't mean you're a failure. You're still far ahead of where you were a year ago, and hopefully along the way you discovered some strengths you didn't know you had.

Let's look back at the year as a whole and figure out where you go from here.

What went well?

Which of your annual goals were not accomplished? Why?

What are your strengths?

What do you need to improve?

What steps can you take to make those needed changes?

What do you think are your barriers? What is standing in your way?

What negative self-talk is sabotaging you? How are your actions undermining your goals? Are those barriers you listed real, or are they imaginary?

Soar

How can you make a start toward overcoming your barriers and mental blocks?

What outside help can you get in order to achieve your goals?

What additional training would help you improve your work performance?

Assuming you pushed past those limitations, what could you accomplish in the next five years?

Soar

Now I want you to dream big. Think about the next twelve months ahead. Use the space below to finish this sentence: "Next year, I want to –"

Congratulations!
You're ready to soar to new heights next year. Make your dreams take wing!

Soar
NEXT YEAR EVENTS CALENDAR

January	February	March

July	August	September

Soar

April	May	June

October	November	December

Soar

Soar

Soar

Soar

Soar

Soar

Soar

About the Press

Eagle Heights Press, a division of *Eagle Heights LLC.*, publishes thriller, fantasy, science fiction, historical fiction, paranormal romance, speculative fiction, young adult, non-fiction, and more.

Find us on the web at eagleheightspress.com.

www.ingramcontent.com/pod-product-compliance
Lightning Source LLC
Chambersburg PA
CBHW030147100526
44592CB00009B/154